T0196720

MY DEAREST
CHRISTINA

MY DEAREST
CHRISTINA

A Father Remembers his Daughter
and her Battle with Lupus

THOMAS O. P. SWEENEY

MY DEAREST CHRISTINA
A FATHER REMEMBERS HIS DAUGHTER
AND HER BATTLE WITH LUPUS

iUniverse books may be ordered through booksellers or by contacting:

iUniverse
1663 Liberty Drive
Bloomington, IN 47403
www.iuniverse.com
1-800-Authors (1-800-288-4677)

Because of the dynamic nature of the Internet, any web addresses or links contained in this book may have changed since publication and may no longer be valid. The views expressed in this work are solely those of the author and do not necessarily reflect the views of the publisher, and the publisher hereby disclaims any responsibility for them.

Any people depicted in stock imagery provided by Thinkstock are models, and such images are being used for illustrative purposes only. Certain stock imagery © Thinkstock.

ISBN: 978-1-5320-3109-0 (sc)
ISBN: 978-1-5320-3110-6 (e)

Library of Congress Control Number: 2017913063

Print information available on the last page.

iUniverse rev. date: 08/30/2017

AUTHOR'S NOTE

I HAD MANY REASONS FOR WRITING this book. I wanted to create a meaningful tribute to my daughter. I wanted to have something tangible for all who knew her to remember her by. I don't think she will ever be forgotten, but hopefully having something like this will be a comfort to her family, friends, co-workers, patients and neighbors.

I believe that this book can also offer some comfort to those who have lost someone. If that includes you, trust me, I feel your pain and your loss. I grieve with you. Your loved one's story cannot be exactly the same as Christina's, but the end is the same. The loss and pain are the same. I hope this helps. You are not alone.

Before 2008 I knew nothing about Lupus. I was vaguely aware that is was some kind of disease. I had no idea that it was such a devastating and cruel disease. My dear hope is that this book will make others aware of Lupus and encourage them to extend sympathy and support to its victims.

I think folks might like to meet Christina. She was a special lady and can and should be an inspiration as she embodied a life well lived.

Finally, and to be perfectly honest, I wrote this book for me. It was important for me to get my emotions on paper. It was a healing labor of love.

I hope I was successful in achieving at least some of these objectives.

Tom Sweeney
Frisco, TX
June 2017

AKNOWLEDGEMENTS

I WANT TO THANK MONSIGNOR WILLIAM Hitpas and Aaron Goldberg for their efforts in editing and proof reading this manuscript. Their help was invaluable.

The subtitle of this book is "A Father Remembers......" It is full of the words "me" and "I". That is because it is a first person narrative. I would be totally remiss if I did not give the major credit for this book to my beautiful bride, Jennifer. She is the one with the caring, kindness, loving and sharing genes which she passed on to Christina. She and Christina were best friends. They were confidants and collaborators. Jennifer is the reason that creep approached me in the coffee shop. She is the reason that Christina "qualified for his employer's services". Jennifer is hurting deeply at the loss of Christina, as am I. I promise we will get through this as we have all of the other difficulties we have faced. Together. Thank you from the bottom of my heart. I love you, Babe.

THE COFFEE SHOP

My daughter, Christina, always liked a particular yuppie coffee shop. She spoke the language which is still incomprehensible to me. A large black coffee is a large black coffee, not some pretentious, mystical mish mass of foreign and English words. When going to visit her during her illness, I often pulled into the shop near her house and ordered her favorite at the drive through window. I would then "surprise" her (not really) when I walked through her door with her favorite beverage. I would normally be rewarded with a thumbs up and a smile warm enough to make glaciers melt.

Christina was the light and joy of my life, and she died early one January morning. The pain and grief I felt were unbearable. It was as if someone reached in and pulled out my heart. I wandered aimlessly along not really seeing or caring. I just tried to get through each day. It was what I imagined existence in a gulag in Siberia was like. One miserable day after another. Get up, muddle through it, and go to bed. Repeat, repeat, repeat! It was like Hell on a treadmill. It was impossible to get off. The pain is as intense now, six months later, as it was when she died.

One morning shortly after her death I just had to get away, so I went for a drive. I was driving through a part of town I had not been to before. It was a bright, sunny day in January, although the temperature mandated wearing a coat. I passed one of the yuppie coffee shops. For some incomprehensible reason I pulled into the parking lot and went inside. I went to the counter and ordered a large black coffee. The kid behind the counter looked at me with a lost stare on his face. After several awkward seconds he told me that they did not have that on the menu. I was shocked. Not being known for my patience, I wanted to lash out verbally at him, but fortunately I was able to refrain myself (barely). I was able to convince him to verify with his manager the fact that they didn't serve black coffee.

The young man returned in a few minutes and admonished me for using the wrong terminology, and that they did in fact have what I wanted, albeit under a different and very strange sounding name. He further went on to inform me that not many people order my selection. Most go for the more exotic concoctions. After an interminable wait, my coffee appeared at the other side of the counter. I surrendered, walked to the other side of the counter, meekly retrieved my large black coffee and looked for an open table to sit and think.

The coffee shop was about half full and reasonably quiet. I went to an empty table, sat down and mindlessly sipped my large black coffee. I honestly didn't even taste it. I started to pray to Christina and for Christina. I cussed out God for taking her, for all of her pain and suffering in her life, and for all the pain those of us left behind were experiencing. Why? Why? Why? Mostly I was just staring straight ahead. People in the shop must have thought I was in a trance.

My eyes were closed when I heard a voice asking if the seat opposite me was taken. Two things surprised me. The first was that there were some, not many, empty tables in the shop. Seating was not at a premium. The second being I am not what most people would consider approachable. I am a hard ass. I don't play well with others. I opened my eyes to see a man of about fifty standing before me. He was one of those people who radiate likability like George Clooney or Tom Hanks. I honestly don't remember anything else about him: height, weight, color of eyes or hair, nothing other than that he was likeable. I was in no mood for likability. I wanted silence and solace. I pointedly glanced about to some of the empty tables, but this guy did not pick up on my subtle suggestion. Without waiting for an official response from me like "get away from me" or "go play in traffic" he pulled out the chair opposite me and sat down.

I cradled the cup of coffee in both hands and shut my eyes willing him to get bored and leave. I have no idea how long I remained like that, but it seemed a good while. I finally opened my eyes and there he was just like before, sitting there looking at me. He said that he knew I had just lost my daughter and that I was experiencing pure agony. I just looked at the guy, not believing he was actually intruding, uninvited, upon my space. Oblivious to the hostility that I was sending in his direction, he said he could help me. I ignored him. The last thing I wanted or needed at that moment was to hear religious verses or platitudes about Christina being in a better place. How the heck would this clown know? Undaunted, he said that he worked for someone who specialized in cases like this. I remember thinking "cases like what?"

He flashed a wide smile on me and said that I should be proud that Christina met all of the criteria necessary to qualify for his employer's service. He explained that his employer was on the lookout for people who were grieving after a qualified loved one departed this earth. Not everyone who passed away qualified for this service. In fact the percentage of those who qualified was unbelievably low.

I'm thinking "OK, here it comes, the sales pitch." He must

have read my mind. He chuckled and told me to relax. There was no fee for his services. His employer had the ability go back in time and erase people. That is not erasing the memory of a person to ease the pain. It is erasing the person, period. Erasing the memory still leaves traces that cause pain and longing and applies only to one person. Others who knew the deceased will still feel pain. By erasing the person, that person never existed. No one misses her. No one feels pain. Life goes on. Since I am Christina's father I was in a position to agree to this service. All I had to do was agree then he would disappear and Christina never existed. I sighed deeply, picked up my coffee, closed my eyes, and wished to God that this creep would leave me alone.

THE EARLY YEARS - O'FALLON & SHILOH, ILLINOIS

Y WIFE JENNIFER (JEN), MY son Tom Jr. (Tommy) and I moved to O'Fallon, Illinois from Fort Hood, TX in 1979 after I resigned my commission from the Army. O'Fallon and the neighboring village of Shiloh are about 15 miles due east of St. Louis, MO along Interstate 64. They are bedroom communities for St. Louis with many of the inhabitants working in downtown St. Louis.

Jen is 100% Italian. Both sides of her family came from small villages located near Rome. Her parents, Frank and Rose, were born near Pittsburgh, PA. All of the women in Jen's family are stubborn and headstrong. They also must possess a special gene. They all started out with beautiful dark brown hair, and none of them ever had a gray hair. The same cannot be said of the men in the family.

Tommy was a wonderful, happy little boy. He was extremely smart and energetic. There was nothing he would not attempt. He carried these traits into adulthood and also added honesty and hard work to them. He was and is a wonderful son. He is a combination of Irish and Italian. His brown hair was originally straight. It became curly in his teens and then started to straighten out as he got older. He does not possess the special gene. He is starting to sprout gray hair.

I vividly remember that day in April. It was around 3 PM and I was in the chemical plant where I worked. Specifically, I was in one of the labs. My pager went off (this was well before cell phones, PC's, and all of the other wonders we take for granted today). I went to the land line and dialed the receptionist. She transferred a phone call to me from my wife, Jennifer. Jennifer was crying. She was distraught. Jennifer was also 9 months pregnant. She ran a pre-school program in the mornings. She planned to close it down for the year in early May when the baby arrived. I finally got a chance, in between sobs, to ask her what was wrong. She replied that she had just returned from an appointment with her OBGYN and that "The baby is coming, and **I'm not ready**." I almost dropped the phone laughing. Her doctor told her that the baby had progressed and that he wanted to take it by C-section the next morning. This was in direct contravention to Jen's plans concerning her pre-school. Jen was a "super teacher", always was and always will be. I told her to take a deep breath and relax. I would be home shortly and we would figure everything out.

I arrived home later that day. Jen's mom was there taking care of our son, Tom Jr. She told me Jen had finally calmed down. I went in and gave Jen a hug. She told me she was to report to the hospital that evening to be admitted, so they could take the baby first thing in the morning. She had accepted the fact that school ended early that year. She had called the lady who was helping her, and together they had called all of the parents whose children were enrolled and informed them of that fact. After dinner I drove Jen to Barnes Hospital in St. Louis where she was admitted. After getting her settled in her room, I kissed her and said goodnight.

The next morning I arrived at Barnes early in the morning. While Jen was being prepped for surgery, I went into a locker room and put on a set of scrubs. I emerged and was escorted to the operating room where I found Jen laying on the table. She had a spinal block for anesthesia, so she was awake the entire time. I was placed in a chair right next to Jen's head. The doctor came in and the procedure started. I could not see what was going on since I was on the wrong side of the barrier around the incision site. At one point one of the folks in the OR came up behind me, put his hands underneath my shoulders and moved me to a standing position. Just then I saw a little baby appear out of the wound. Not knowing the sex prior to the birth, I exuberantly announced to everyone in the OR and to the world, "It's a girl". Jen and I were the proud parents of a beautiful little girl.

I left Jen and Christina an hour or so later and went to work for a short while. I then went home and told Mema, Jen's mom, and Tommy that we had a new little girl in the family. Tommy said, "I'm glad I have a baby 'ister.'" We had an early dinner, and then the three of us drove into St. Louis to meet Christina. We walked down the corridor in the direction of the nursery. Mema moved ahead of us and one glace at all of the babies behind the glass was all it took. She immediately pointed out Christina. She didn't need to read the tags on the cribs. She just knew. This was the start of a bond and love affair that would last until Mema's death in 2012.

Over the next two or so days, the three of us would go in daily to visit Jen and Christina. Jen remarked that Christina was a wonderful baby. She slept the entire time she was in the room with Jen. We were soon to find out that she had her days and nights mixed up. She was up all night partying and giving the nurses a run for their money. Once we got her home, it was Mema who finally got her on the right schedule. The love of partying was never cured. Christina loved to party and have a good time.

Christina and Jen

Christina and Mema

Mema was a stubborn and headstrong lady. She also went through life with the unshakable certainty that she never made a mistake. As a very young girl, Christina was hardheaded and stubborn. People would say that she was a lot like Rose, a.k.a. Mema. Rose would get irate at this comparison and exclaim that she was nowhere near as stubborn. Christina on the other hand would get extremely mad when I called her "Little Mema". Truth be told, they were two peas in a pod. They totally adored each other.

When Christina was about five years old, she had a shirt that was covered with pictures of Mickey Mouse in various moods. There must have been fifty or sixty pictures of Mickey exhibiting different emotions ranging from ecstatic happiness to inconsolable sadness with everything in-between. I'll never forget the time Christina got mad about something. She looked at me, pointed to a picture on her shirt of "mad Mickey" and said: "See this Mickey. He's mad, and so am I." I almost died laughing which made her even madder.

Christina was by no means perfect. She exhibited all of the characteristics of a normal young girl growing up in America's Heartland. She had her good points and points that yearned for improvement. She had a mischievous streak. Once while she was still a toddler, this streak manifested itself. We lived in a split foyer house. One Saturday morning I was downstairs with the two kids, and Jen was upstairs in the kitchen. Tommy was playing with blocks, constructing a rather tall building. I looked over at Christina and saw that she had this evil gleam in her eye. I knew she was up to no good. Sure enough, she crawled over towards Tommy. When he wasn't looking she pounced and knocked over his building. Before anyone could do anything, she started crying and screaming for Tommy to stop hitting her. The poor guy was just sitting there in shock. He hadn't touched her or even yelled at her. Jen, upstairs, heard the commotion and immediately started yelling down at Tommy. Christina stopped her wailing and a smile came onto her face. At this point I stepped in and put things right. Christina got yelled at. Jen got yelled at. Tommy got praised for his restraint.

Christina also exhibited a very caring side at a young age. This trait would characterize her for her entire life. When she was five or six years old, she was enrolled in ballet lessons. Her dance school was performing *Cinderella* for the end of the year recital. The younger girls had a number called *Dream Cinderella* in which the older girl who had the title role danced with the younger girls. One of the younger girls was chosen to play the part of Cinderella as a young girl. She was in a different costume from the others and had a short solo. Christina wanted this role and worked very hard at her dancing. The dance class met every Saturday morning. I remember picking her up after class one morning. As we were driving home, she quietly told me that she got the part. I was excited and thrilled for her and told her so. I could tell she was happy, but something was wrong. She finally said that another little girl also wanted the part. When the teacher announced that Christina had the part, the other girl broke down and cried. Christina felt terrible about this. She hated to see others disappointed and hurt. I tried to explain that no one can win every time. She went out, did her best, and today her best was good enough. At another time, the other little girl's best would win her the role or position she was trying for. A person does his or her best and hopes for the best. I don't know if I helped Christina, but she seemed to accept what I was saying. What struck me then, and it's something I have never forgotten, was her compassion for another even at the moment where she had won a victory and could be celebrating.

Dream Cinderella

Christina developed a deep faith in God. She was a devoted Catholic. We were blessed to join a new parish that started up when Christina was two years old. When the parish first started, Masses were held in the Knights of Columbus hall. Everyone sat on folding chairs and the altar was a folding table. Construction of the new church took almost two years. We would go to Mass every Sunday and Christina would always sit on my lap. She usually made it to the *Gloria* before falling fast asleep. I used to tease the pastor, our dear friend Father Bill Hitpas, that Christina was well into her twenties before she stayed awake to hear his homilies. That of course is an exaggeration. Father Bill watched Christina grow up and turn into the beautiful person she ultimately became. He selected her while she was in first grade to carry the Baby Jesus figure to the crib during the procession starting Christmas Eve Mass. About five years later, she was selected to be the Virgin Mary in a Christmas pageant run by The Parish School of Religion.

Christina was a wonderful student. Her grades were excellent. I remember her sobbing when she was a junior in high school. She received her first B on a report card. I held her tight and said that most kids would kill for a B. That didn't make it better for her, but I think it put the B somewhat into perspective. As I recall that was the only B she received in high school. She really excelled in science and math and wanted to pursue a career in a science based field.

Christina made friends easily. More importantly, the friends she made remained her friends during her entire life. She cared deeply about them. Sometimes her caring nature got her in trouble. One of her girlfriends from elementary school moved away. She returned in her late teens with a boyfriend and not much hope for success. One evening she called Christina at home to tell her that they had been in a car accident. Christina immediately dropped everything and went to the rescue despite my telling her to stay home. She returned an hour or so later and announced that she had been pulled over for speeding. Needless to say, I lost it. I went right through the roof. Jen on the other hand knew exactly what to do. It seems that Jennifer had been pulled over by the Shiloh Chief of Police numerous times for speeding. Each time she had been able to get away with a warning. She called the Chief and explained what happened with Christina and why. The chief came over to our home that evening. He lectured and admonished Christina about driving more carefully and reduced the ticket to a warning.

Another chapter in her misadventure with friends concerned the time one of her lifelong friends got a job at a local fast food restaurant. She convinced Christina to apply for a summer job there. Christina did so and was hired. As a prejudiced observer, in my humble opinion many of Christina's co-workers were not playing with full decks. Several had either left home or were asked to leave by their parents. These kids were hopeless and hapless. Christina knew she could help them. She looked on them like stray puppies. It got to the point when I awoke in the morning, my first stop was to check the spare bedroom. More often than not there would be a strange boy sleeping there. My routine never changed. I went downstairs and counted the silverware, woke up the sleeping beauty, put him in my car and deposited him far away from my home. When I would confront Christina she would always say that the kid just needed a little help, and she wanted to provide it. Fortunately the summer finally ended, and Christina left her job. No one was hurt, and nothing was stolen.

As happens with most teenage girls, they have a period where they are self-absorbed. Christina could have been the poster girl for this phenomena. She had no time for her family. Everything revolved around her and her friends. She was moody and irritable. I called her a "constipated rattle snake". She lived on the phone. This was before cell phones, so our land line at home was constantly tied up. On one occasion I went on a business trip to Orlando. I stayed the Peabody Hotel. It was a very nice hotel. They charged you every time you dialed the phone. I had a company phone card, and I had a habit of calling home every night while I was on the road. I called home and the line was busy. I repeated this for at least an hour and a half. I finally got through, and I was one unhappy camper. Christina had been in her room talking with a friend. Jen didn't notice the phone was gone. The following day when I went to check out of the hotel I became even more furious. The Peabody presented me with a bill for $80. They charge for each call made whether it goes through or not. A quick word with the hotel manager rectified the problem, but still, the experience was painful and frustrating.

Christina considered becoming a veterinarian. She also considered going to medical school. She finally settled on pharmacy as a career. Initially she thought she wanted to go to the University of Michigan, but she was willing to consider other schools. Tom was enrolled at Purdue University; was doing well; and he loved it there. Christina, Jennifer and I had made many trips to Purdue to see Tom and to go to football games and other functions. She was familiar with the school and put it on her list of possibles. During the summer between her junior and senior year, we went on the pilgrimage to visit the schools on her list. She said we didn't need to visit Purdue since she was already familiar with it. I insisted we go there. She was familiar with it as an outsider visiting her brother. She needed to visit it as a prospective student and see it from a different perspective. She reluctantly agreed, and we made the trek there. The School of Pharmacy, which was ranked among the very best in the country, put on a very impressive presentation. Our next stop was the University of Notre Dame. She quickly excluded it from her list. She was not at all comfortable there. Our final stop was The University of Michigan. Michigan has multiple campuses and freshmen need to be bussed between them. We also noticed that there were emergency call boxes located all over campus. I asked the tour guide about this. She replied that they had a few incidents but not more than normal. Neither Jen, Christina nor I could recall seeing emergency call boxes at Purdue. We left Michigan and started to drive home. We were just outside of Fort Wayne, IN when Christina announced she wanted to go to Purdue. All three of us in the car were excited and very comfortable with her choice.

PURDUE UNIVERSITY

J ENNIFER AND I DROPPED OFF a "constipated rattlesnake" at Purdue in August 1998. We were up several times for visits during her first semester, and she seemed the same as normal. Something happened that first semester. I am not sure what. The person who came home for Christmas vacation that year was the most wonderful, loving, considerate, caring, generous, friendly (you get the general idea) person ever created. I joke that Christina's fairy godmother hit her upside of her head with her magic wand, but the reality was that she grew up. It was a true metamorphosis.

Christina was made for Purdue and Purdue was made for her. She loved to study and she loved to party. Few people can excel at both, but she did. Her grades were outstanding from the very beginning which was no real surprise. She became a member of Pi Beta Phi sorority at the start of second semester of her freshman year. She was able to perfectly balance the sorority life with the intense demands of the Pharm D program. She once remarked to me that she had to work very hard not to be a nerd. Christina's sorority sisters became lifelong friends. They truly loved each other.

STL Mardi Gras with Meagan (Pi Beta Phi), Julie (K-12 grade)

STL Mardi Gras with Chicago Flat Mates

Early in her freshman year, Christina met a young man at Purdue who was from the Chicago area. His name was Aaron Goldberg. Both Jennifer and I liked him very much. Aaron was a year ahead of her. They started dating. We knew he was special, because he could withstand visits from Mema who by then was saying more than her prayers. He was able to laugh about the experience and not take offence. They dated for the entire time at school and became engaged just before she graduated. They got married in 2005 with Father Bill and a rabbi doing the honors at a joint Jewish/Catholic wedding uniting Aaron and Christina Goldberg.

The Wedding Kiss

The Beautiful Bride with Dad

When I walked Christina down the aisle, I was brimming with pride and also sadness. My little girl was moving on. When we got to the chuppah, I held Christina's hand and gave her a kiss on her cheek. I whispered to her to "take care of him". Christina looked me in the eye and firmly nodded her head and promised that she would. I turned and shook hands with Aaron and said "take care of her". Aaron looked me in the eye and firmly nodded his head and promised that he would. I then took Christina's hand and placed it in Aaron's and said "take care of each other". Three promises were made then, and there have never been promises better kept than these three. They took care of each other and supported each other in good times as well as bad. There were times I am sure lesser folks would have cut and run. Not so Aaron and Christina. They held fast, and they held firm, and they held each other. They were an example and inspiration to their family and to their friends.

The Happy Couple

The Pharm D program at Purdue is six years. The first five are on campus. The final year is an externship where the candidate works in different pharmacy related fields at off campus locations. The students were allowed to request a city or location where they would like to do their externship. Christina could have picked St. Louis where she could have lived at home and saved me money. But NOOO, she picked Chicago which was where Aaron was living and working. It was also the Chicago of high rents and high cost of living. She found a beautiful apartment with two other young women just off of Belmont about 5 blocks from Wrigley Field. This was definitely high end yuppie country. I might add that Christina's two flat mates both were working and bringing in pay checks. My little beauty relied on the 'Bank of Dad'. As an aside, I should note that after she graduated and was out in the workforce, the first thing she did was find another apartment. The new place was only one or two blocks from her old one, but comparatively speaking, it was a dump. Jen and I asked why she had chosen to move out of her beautiful apartment and into one totally lacking in amenities. She looked at us like we were nuts and said, "Because the 'Bank of Dad' closed."

Graduation Day 2004

CHICAGO

THE ENTIRE AREA WHERE SHE lived was vibrant and upbeat. A very beautiful Catholic Church, Our Lady of Mount Carmel, was only six or seven blocks away. Christina joined the parish and set out to become involved in it. She became a Eucharistic Minister and truly loved being part of the liturgy. It was at this time when she discovered she had a gluten allergy. She continued as a Eucharistic Minister but limited herself to only handling the wine.

It was during her time in Chicago where Christina really learned to be a pharmacist. She worked for Walgreens and soon took ownership and responsibility for "her" store. She loved working with the staff and especially loved working with her patients. She developed a rapport with them that made them loyal Walgreens' customers.

Aaron and Christina loved kids. They volunteered to mentor some of the underprivileged young people in the surrounding community. They worked on academic skills as well as fun things like swimming and playing ball.

During Christina's fifth year at Purdue, her final year on campus, Aaron bought her a puppy. Eddie was an Australian Shepherd and became the love of her life. He was smart as a whip and developed skills in opening doors and locks that would have make Houdini proud. And he LOVED the water. There was a puppy beach located at the end of Belmont in Lake Michigan. This beach was only a few blocks from Our Lady of Mount Carmel, so it was an easy walk from either of her two apartments. During hot summer days Christina and Aaron would take Eddie to the beach. He would swim out pretty far and hated to leave the water when called to go home. He was like a big, hairy duck. Poor Eddie also loved food like no other animal I ever saw. It was an obsession to him. This in part could be explained by Christina being a health conscious owner. She was bound and determined that Eddie would not get fat. Eddie would get his dish of food in the morning and in the evening. He devoured it immediately and then looked for more. If he spied another dog eating he became unbearable. He would growl and carry on like a big hairy baby.

Jack, Eddie, Christina and Aaron

High Five with Eddie

Christina, Eddie and Jack

After they were married, Aaron and Christina moved to Ukrainian Village, a neighborhood in Chicago. They purchased a condo on a quiet street. They also bought another Australian Shepherd who they named Jack. While Eddie was black with a few tan markings on his snout, rear end and legs, Jack was a beautiful light tan color. The first thing Aaron and Christina did with Jack was to send him to "Puppy University" for two weeks of training. He graduated "summa cum doggy". I made the mistake of including this in my annual Christmas letter along with the fact that even though Jack had advanced degrees, he was still a regular guy. He interacted with other dogs with lesser education and was happy to sniff their tails. Well the wrath of Christina fell squarely on her old Dad. It took her weeks before she settled down.

Speaking of the wrath of Christina, there is the story of the Christmas jewelry. When she was a little girl of five or six, Christina wanted to get her ears pierced. Her fuddy-duddy dad thought this was a barbaric practice and forbad it. I was successful for a while in preventing this, but the constant withering attacks were taking their toll. I knew I was fighting a losing battle. That Christmas I went to the jewelry store and bought her a pair of diamond studs. She was thrilled. The day after Christmas she went with her mom and aunt to complete the deed. She came home a happy young lady. End of story, right? Nope! Just before the following Christmas she reminded me that she expected jewelry from Dad. She liked getting the earrings so much that she thought that this was a tradition that should continue. And continue it did. I would normally go to a jewelry store in early December and get her something. Several times Jen would help me or actually pick out the piece herself. Christina could always tell when Dad had help picking her gift. Some were elegant and beautiful while others were dowdy and practical. I won't say which was which. Now to the wrath. After she got married, I stupidly thought that Aaron would assume the duty of buying the Christmas jewelry for her. That Christmas there was no box from dad. Aaron got her a very nice present, but that did not cut it. Tradition is tradition. She now had two men in her life and both were irreplaceable but not interchangeable. Certain things were Aaron's jobs and certain things were Dad's. Period. End of story. She made me feel so guilty that on Valentine's Day I presented her with a piece of jewelry that was elegant, beautiful **AND** very expensive. I returned to her good graces, and I learned my lesson. She received a piece of jewelry every Christmas thereafter.

Christmas 2005, the year with no "Daddy Jewelry" (The Whole Clan)

Christmas 2005, the year with no "Daddy
Jewelry" (Aaron and Christina)

Christina loved to run. And run she did. She often took both
Eddie and Jack on leashes for long runs through the streets of
Chicago. Distances of five to ten miles or even more were not
uncommon.

She also developed a love for cooking while in Chicago. She
became a very good cook and prepared many gourmet dishes.
She would watch cooking shows on television while running
on her tread mill. She loved to entertain and show off her
culinary skills. I might add that she did all of that after she'd
discovered she had a gluten allergy. She could not enjoy many
of the delicious dishes she'd prepare; however, it did not stop
her from cooking. She enjoyed the pleasure her cooking gave
to all of her lucky guests.

Chef Christina in chef's outfit, a Christmas present from Aaron

Aaron's mother, Marla, was very ill for a time. She has since recovered. One year at Passover, Aaron and Christina invited the Goldberg's over for dinner. Aaron's family lived in near-by Arlington Heights, IL. Marla insisted that Aaron and Christina just serve a regular meal. Christina went on the internet and looked up directions for the Passover Seder. When Marla, Aaron's father, Ted, and brother, Seth, arrived for dinner, Christina had the special meal prepared. This made a lasting impression on Aaron's family.

Christina truly was respectful of Aaron's faith. December was a time for two religious celebrations: Christmas and Hanukkah. The house would be decorated jointly for both feasts. She even went so far as to buy Santa and Hanukkah outfits for both her and Aaron as well as Eddie and Jack. Eddie was the rabbi and Jack was Santa. It was hilarious.

December Holidays at the Goldberg's

One day as Christina entered her building, she saw an envelope laying on the concrete. She picked it up and opened it. It contained over $400. There was no address or other identification on the envelope, so she had no good way to return it to its owner. She asked around the building if anyone had lost an envelope. No one had. She contacted the local police precinct to report that she had found a sum of money. (She did turn down their offer to watch the money for her.) They told her no one reported a loss, and they would let her know if and when someone did report it. She let several months pass and contacted the police again. They told her that it was highly unlikely anyone would come forward at this late date to claim the money and that she could keep it. Again Christina's selfless character came to the forefront. She took part of the money and bought new purses for her mother and Jenny, Tom Jr's wife. She gave the remainder to Father Elmer at her parish church. She strove always to make others happy.

Christina and Aaron had a desire to give to the community. They read about a fund raising triathlon to benefit the Leukemia and Lymphoma Society. To participate in the triathlon each team had to raise a $3,000 entry fee. They proceeded to contact friends and neighbors for donations as sponsors for their team. They hosted a Texas Holdem poker night. I was disappointed in the poker night, not because I lost, but because of reaction of the participants. Aaron and Christina spent a small fortune on drinks and snacks. The entry fee they charged barely covered their expenses. At the end of the day, the winners pocketed their winnings and left. No one made a donation to the charity. A lot of hard work and effort was spent with really nothing to show for it.

Now begins a very sad chapter in my precious little girl's life. It was a Saturday morning a week or so before the triathlon was scheduled. Christina woke up with a splitting headache, a very sore neck and an aversion to light. It had the earmarks of meningitis. She called her family physician who immediately sent her to the emergency room at Northwestern University Hospital. The doctors there ordered a spinal tap. In the process of performing the procedure something went wrong and a nerve was touched. She was in excruciating pain. She was admitted to the hospital, and for several weeks no one was sure if the pain she was experiencing was the disease or the botched spinal tap. The results of the tap were negative for meningitis. She was eventually released from the hospital. She returned home but her hopes of competing in the triathlon were forever dashed. Aaron went to the organizers of the competition to withdraw their team. They gave him the bicycle shorts and jerseys that they would have worn in the meet. My heart broke when Christina and Aaron came out to the living room of their house to model the attire that they would never use.

The doctors at Northwestern were not sure what was wrong with Christina, so we traveled to the south side of Chicago to the University of Chicago Hospital. Again the doctor there was unable to diagnose the problem. For the next several months Christina tried to get on with her life. She returned to work and made the best of things. Occasionally she would be in so much pain she needed to be readmitted to Northwestern Hospital. On one of these stays a rheumatologist finally made the tentative diagnosis of Lupus. I say tentative because the disease is very hard to diagnose and presents itself in many forms.

At last we had a name for it, so Aaron made an appointment with Mayo Clinic in Rochester, MN. Jen and I drove there in December 2008 and met Aaron and Christina at the hotel. I think we were expecting "super docs" who could and would cure anything. That did not happen. The process at Mayo is that the patient first sees the equivalent of a general practitioner who then refers the patient to the appropriate specialists. We saw the GP who then made or tried to make appointments with the specialists. On some days we would see several doctors, on other days none. She saw a dermatologist to check out the rash she developed on her face. The doctor did a biopsy of the rash. Unfortunately the lab lost the sample so there were no results. This was typical of what Christina was encountering. If she did not have bad luck, she would have had no luck at all. The key doctor we wanted to see was a rheumatologist, but this doctor did not have any appointments available. We were told we could take a chance and sit in his waiting room and perhaps his staff could fit us in. We did, and fortunately they did. Again there were no definitive eurekas or silver bullets. The rheumatologist did give Christina some advice. He told her he had patients who just retreated and curled up into balls and died. He told her she had to fight like hell to get her life back. She took this advice to heart and fight she did. She was a furious warrior.

Christina and Aaron returned to Chicago and resumed their lives. Christina endured the pain, but continued to run and make the best of things. They purchased a new vehicle, an Acura SUV. It was beautiful. Their garage was a separate building behind the condo and was shared by all of the owners in the complex. People speculated that one of the owners was into something he should not have been, and a drug deal went bad. In retaliation, the aggrieved party set fire to the garage. It was destroyed. The brand new Acura SUV was totaled two weeks after they drove it home. Their insurance company covered the replacement cost, but the sales tax was lost. That was several thousand dollars down the drain. The lucky streak was obviously still intact.

While summers in Chicago are glorious, the winters are brutal. That is stating the obvious. The weather exacerbated the pain of Christina's condition. The couple decided to move to Texas. Christina's brother, Tom Jr., and his wife, Jenny, lived just outside of Dallas. So Aaron and Christina had friendly faces and a base to operate out of while they looked for a new home. Both of their employers, Walgreens and Blue Cross/Blue Shield, were agreeable for them to transfer to their respective facilities outside of Dallas. Aaron and Christina had a house built for them in Lewisville, TX and made the move to Texas in September of 2010.

TEXAS

THE HOUSE, LOCATED IN THE Castle Hills subdivision of Lewisville, was quite a house: two stories, 5 bedrooms, 4 bathrooms, a game room, a media room, etc., etc. It had all the bells and whistles one could hope for. They filled it with beautiful furnishings, and even more importantly, they filled it with their hopes and dreams. My heart breaks when I think of what might have been.

Aaron settled in to his new office in Richardson, TX. It was about a thirty-five minute drive from his home to the office. Given the traffic situation in and around the Dallas/Fort Worth area, a thirty-five minute drive was not bad at all. Christina also started at her new store which was also located in Richardson. This was very convenient, and sometimes they were able to ride together when their work schedules meshed.

Christina had learned the basics of being a pharmacist while working in Chicago. In Texas she perfected it. After a short while as a staff pharmacist she was promoted to pharmacy manager. She took to this like a duck to water. She was demanding of herself and her staff. Her patients came first. Not long after she moved to Texas, Walgreens moved her from one Richardson store to another. I personally don't pay attention to whom my pharmacist is. Not so Christina's patients. Many transferred their medicines the new store. I certainly don't bring my pharmacist cards or flowers. When Christina returned to work after one of her hospital stays she was greeted with many cards and flowers.

One of her patients wrote a letter to the CEO of Walgreens that was full of glowing praise for my daughter. Something intrigued the CEO who sent a professional photographer to take some photos of her. Evidently the CEO liked what he saw. He then sent in a video crew who shot a video of Christina and her staff at work In the video, Christina related a story about how by spending a little time with a patient, she was able to figure out what was causing the problems this young mother was experiencing and how to correct them. She emphasized patient relations in the short video. The CEO really liked what he saw and this video was placed on the company's intranet for training purposes.

Not only did Christina show the utmost care and respect for her patients, on occasion she paid for their medicines when they needed them and could not afford them. Obviously she could not afford to do this often, but in special cases she did step in and cover the costs out of her own pocket.

As the disease progressed, Jen and I realized that our place was with Christina in Texas. I had worked for the same company in Illinois for 36 years, and the company was in the process of phasing out operations there over the next year or so. In 2015 they were not quite ready to close and needed help with the transition from Illinois to Houston. I was asked what my plans were vis-a-vis retirement. I replied that I would be willing to stay with the company for another year and retire at age 66 if I could work from home, and by the way, home was going to be in Texas. Since all I needed to do my job was a computer, a high speed internet connection and a phone, the company agreed. Jen and I built a home in Frisco, TX about six miles from Christina and relocated

to Texas in October 2015. From then on either Jen or I would be at Christina's almost every day. I drove her to most of her many doctors' appointments. We did our best to support her in every possible way.

My daughter tried to do at least one act of kindness every day. I obviously do not know about them all, and even if I did, I would not be able to relate all of them here. There are several rather poignant examples that I witnessed that made me marvel. Lupus is an autoimmune disease. As the name implies the immune system is compromised. Christina contracted a series of very serious infections along the way and had to see numerous infectious disease specialists to battle these deadly infections. Often the ID doctor would insert a PICC line to facilitate the delivery of the antibiotics. On one visit to her ID doctor's office, we encountered an older gentleman. His PICC line was visible as was Christina's. They looked at each other like kindred spirits as we rode the elevator. Upon entering the office, Christina checked in with the receptionist and was told to take a seat. The older gentleman was not so fortunate. The lady behind the desk informed him that he did not have an appointment. This greatly upset the man who evidently had driven from his home about an hour's drive away. He got into an argument with the receptionist who did not exactly exude an abundance of compassion or kindness. I buried my head deeper into the magazine I was reading and hoped this would soon blow over. To my surprise, Christina went over to the man. He at first looked at her as if he wanted to strike out and hit her, then he recognized her as the young lady with the PICC line from the elevator and settled down a bit. Christina spoke to him with empathy and kindness much like she would to her patients. After a few minutes of conversation, and with the reluctant assistance of her majesty, the receptionist, it was apparent that the man did in fact have an appointment, but it was at the doctor's other office

in a different town. He thanked Christina for her kindness and left with his dignity intact.

Jennifer and I joined Holy Cross Parish in The Colony, TX. It was a small church with a great pastor and very nice parishioners. Christina would join us on Sunday mornings when she was feeling up to it. On one Sunday, there was a young man in his twenties with spina bifida sitting in the pew in front of us. I had seen him at Mass before and noticed that he usually sat alone. As we stood for the "Our Father" my family joined hands as is our custom. Christina was at the far end of the pew standing right next to me. She saw this young man sitting alone and looking lonely. She reached out and put her hand on his shoulder while we all said the prayer. The look that came onto his face was magical. He saw this beautiful young woman reaching out to him. He looked like he was gazing at an angel. I think he may have been right. On following Sundays when Christina would join us, I would see this young man making or trying to make eye contact with her and always giving her a big smile which she would happily return.

As I already mentioned, Christina was very religious. She truly loved God. She hated when she missed Mass because of her work schedule and then when the disease took its tool and she physically could not go out. I purchased a **St. Joseph Sunday Missal** when the new liturgy went into effect. On Sundays when she worked, she would call me when she returned home and I would read the entire set of readings, including commentary, to her. We started doing this when she worked in Chicago and continued on with the practice until the end. It was time together that we both came to cherish even if the circumstances were not ideal.

Christina became the queen of texting. She used text messages as a way to reach out to people and show support and

encouragement. My roommate from school has a wife who needed to have a very serious and delicate procedure done to some of the nerves in her head. Christina somehow found out about this and started texting her. The two became fast friends and supported each other greatly in their times of need. I am pleased to report that Marian's procedure was successful, and she made a full recovery. Ray and Marian visited Christina twice while they were in the Dallas area. The first time they found Christina in the hospital in Dallas with her electrolytes out of balance. She was on IV's to stabilize them. This was the first time that they actually met Christina, and the three of them had a very nice visit. Christina was fighting sepsis on their second visit. I took her to an appointment with her infectious disease doctor on the afternoon of Marian and Ray's visit. He told her that she was very gravely ill and needed to be hospitalized immediately. Of course she refused. She told him she would check herself into the hospital later that evening. She had made a breakfast dish for Ray and Marian for the next morning and she was bound and determined to serve it. I drove her back to her house arguing all the way. Shortly after we got home, Ray and Marian arrived. They were appalled by what Christina was doing. After a while we all reached a compromise. We would all visit for an hour or so. After that Ray and Marian plus the French toast for breakfast would head to our house for dinner and to spend the night. Aaron would take Christina to the hospital as she promised the doctor. And thus it came to pass that everyone honored their part of the bargain. We all had a very nice visit at Christina's. Christina went to the hospital where she would spend a week battling the infection. Jen, Marian, Ray and I had a very pleasant evening together, and then we had a delicious breakfast the next morning thanks to my gourmet chef.

Christina was in and out of hospitals too many times to count over the last three years of her life. She tried to make the best out of a bad situation. She was very friendly with the aides who were very kind to her. She took an active interest in most of the female nurses who cared for her. She would immediately learn their backgrounds, including whether they were married, and if so, she'd ask if they have children, etc. If the nurse happened to be single, Christina took it as a personal challenge to play matchmaker. She constantly tried to fix those nurses up with some of her single, male friends. She developed friendships with several of the nurses. In some cases the nurse would have to recuse herself (I'm not sure if that is the correct phrase in medicine.) from being assigned as a caregiver to Christina, because she and Christina had become close friends. At shift change it was not uncommon to see several of these nurses who were going off duty entering Christina's room to visit with her.

Christina with Kim, one of her nurses, out shopping

During her hospital stays, she would on occasion get visits from the hospitals' chaplains. They would come to visit her to offer solace and support. The chaplain on one of these visits asked her if she knew about the ministry she was performing. He said she was having a profound impact on the entire staff on the floor. They marveled at the strength and grace she showed even though she was in tremendous pain. She always greeted the staff with a smile and words of encouragement and gratitude for the care they were providing. He said he heard this from doctors, nurses, techs, aides and even the cleaning people on the floor. He thanked her from the bottom of his heart for what she was doing in making the hospital a happier place.

Making people happy was what she was all about. She and Aaron met a young couple originally from Indiana. In fact, both of these folks graduated from Indiana University, the hated in-state rival of Purdue. Proving that Purdue grads could overlook others' faults, they became best friends with Billi and Malachi. Billi and Malachi lived in the same neighborhood about 5 blocks from the Goldberg's. The two couples spent a lot of time together going out to dinner, sporting events, and just enjoying each other's company. One day in early December of 2016, I went to Christina's place to sit with her. I was shocked, worried and surprised when I opened the garage and found her car missing. She was not supposed to drive. I checked the house inside and out and found no trace of her. I sent her a text asking for her whereabouts and thankfully received a reply that she was at Billi's. I drove there expecting to find her inside visiting, but **NO**, she was on her knees in the front yard busily planting 100 tulip bulbs. I lost it. I asked what she thought she was doing, and she replied she wanted to surprise Billi. These plants did come up this spring and made Billi's yard even more beautiful.

I know Billi and Malachi will remember her every spring when the flowers bloom.

Billi

I mentioned that Christina drove the 5 blocks to Billi's house that morning. Before Christina became ill she had the dubious honor being the world's worst driver. She would occupy all six lanes of a two lane road. I pride myself on being an excellent driver, so Christina's lack of ability was a true embarrassment to me. She must have been trained by Jen, so similar were their skills behind the wheel. To get to Christina's garage in Texas, one had to take an alley to the rear of the house. Christina ran over the grass in the alley so many times that the neighborhood association had boulders installed to discourage bad driving. I threatened to have a road sign put up with "Christina's Causeway" printed on it. She did not see the humor in this, so I again experienced the wrath of Christina.

Christina's love of dogs played an important part in her life and the lives of her family members. Jen and I had a wonderful Rat Terrier named Zeus. Zeus was with us for thirteen years. Jen and I went on a European cruise in 2013 for just under two weeks. We put Zeus and our other dog, Maddie, in a very nice kennel while we were gone. The day we returned to the US, we went to pick the guys up at the kennel. The kennel informed us that Zeus had passed away in his sleep while we were away. They did not inform us because we were very far away and there was nothing we could have done. Although we were heartbroken for our loss, we agreed the kennel had done the right thing. A week or so later we received a call from Christina. She was entering a PetSmart to buy something. An animal rescue group had several dogs there they were trying to find homes for. One little guy captured her heart. He was a Shih Tzu/terrier mix with protruding lower teeth. He was a doggy orthodontist's dream. She described him to us and wanted to know if we would like him. She assured us that he was totally loveable. Jen and I knew that the decision had already been made for us, so we agreed. We drove down to Texas a week or so later to visit Aaron and Christina and to meet Harry. Harry was a lover and turned out to be a great addition to our family. He loved Jen and me unconditionally, but he had an incredibly strong bond with Christina. Whenever she was around, Harry was right next to her. He even insisted on sleeping in her bed. Sometimes we felt he was a traitor such was the attraction she had over him.

Christina with Harry

In the fall of 2015, her beloved dog, Eddie, developed cancer. It was heartbreaking. They found a veterinarian who was an oncology specialist. She put Eddie on a regime of very expensive injections to try to slow down the diseases' progression. This treatment was marginally successful, but just before Christmas that year Eddie had to be put down. Jen and I accompanied Aaron and Christina to the vet's office and did our best to console them afterwards. It was a heartbreaking experience for all of us. Not wanting Jack to be alone, they went out and found an Australian Shepherd puppy they named Gus. Gus is a character. When you look at him, even if he is just sitting still, he looks guilty. He was good for Christina. He kept her focused on him and not on what was going on around her. I often found Gus curled up next to her on the couch or in her bed when I arrived for my daily visits.

Jack and Gus (puppy)

She always loved Daddy/Daughter projects as she called them. These were opportunities for us to be together and share some quiet time. Some were as simple as putting jigsaw puzzles together. Others were more complex. We carved pumpkins together ever since she was a little girl. Once she moved to Texas and met Billi, I was the third wheel in pumpkins. The two of them took great pleasure in creating masterpieces. She loved Christmas, and she loved building and decorating gingerbread houses with me. I confess I built the houses and then she and Aaron would decorate them together. That was the best of both worlds for her, spending time with the two men in her life. On the Christmas before she died, she found a Hanukkah House complete with menorahs, dreidels, gold coins and the Star of David. She and I worked on it all day long. When Aaron returned home that evening he had the surprise of his life. Of course I also built a gingerbread house that the two of them could decorate. For another project, she designed an autumn door hanging and enlisted my aid. I went to Home Depot for the supplies and put the hanging together to the point where she could decorate it. We made 3 of them. She took the first to Billi's house and hung it on the door for her to find it when she came home from work. I think Billi was pleased with it, and this in turn pleased Christina to no end.

The Hanukkah House

Autumn Door Hanging

Christina had a severe case of OCD. Everything had to be just so. Her closets had everything perfectly arranged. The pantry in the kitchen had labels on every shelf indicating what went where. God help me if I put the vegetable oil where the olive oil was supposed to be. Her OCD made interactions between Christina and Jen hilarious. Jen's philosophy is "What the heck, close enough". The squabbling that went on when Jen did the laundry for her was priceless. I wish Jen mated my socks with such meticulous care. What the heck, close enough!

Christina and Jen

So much of the final years was taken up with the battle against Lupus. The pain and suffering Christina endured were beyond description, yet she never complained and never openly felt sorry for herself. She accepted what was dealt her with grace and equanimity. I never could have done it. My understanding is that Lupus has no set or standard course. It attacks its victims in a myriad of different ways. With Christina it focused on her GI system. It started by shutting down her stomach. She was not able to eat and keep the food down. Needless to say action had to be taken so that she could receive nutrients and medicine. A "J-tube" was inserted into her intestine. This allowed liquid medication as well as liquid food to be fed into the intestine to be absorbed. We made two more visits to Mayo Clinic in 2015 to see if there was a way to get the stomach restarted. Unfortunately there wasn't. Mayo did insert a "G-tube" in her stomach. This allowed Christina to eat and drink. Whatever she consumed passed directly from the stomach into a bag via the "G-tube". The benefit of this is that she did not vomit which eased the wear and tear on her esophagus and other organs while allowing her the pleasure of tasting real food. She continued to lose weight, but eventually was able to plateau just under 100 pounds.

She had numerous vitamin, hormone and mineral deficiencies. She developed osteoporosis to the point where her endocrinologist told us she had the bones of a 90 year old woman. She was only 33.

One of the most frightening and dangerous development was the onslaught of seizures. She could be walking, standing, sitting or lying down when they occurred without warning. Most of these "just" caused her to pass out. Another variety caused her to become rigid while being unconsciousness. Finally there were the Grand Mal seizures where violent convulsions accompanied the loss of consciousness. These were very dangerous as she could bang her head on the ground and cause serious injury. Aaron, Jen and I made a real effort to have at least one of us with her at all times. On the instances where there was a gap in coverage, I was terrified when I opened the door to her house. I never knew what I would find. One time the four of us went to see the local professional soccer team play. We had just entered the stadium and were walking on a concourse, with Christina walking between Aaron and me, when the seizure hit. Christina went down face first on the concrete. Fortunately she did not injure herself with the fall, but we were all scared.

In my opinion we experienced the good, the bad, and the incompetent with respect to the doctors she saw. Some were caring and compassionate. These doctors over time became visibly frustrated with the lack of success. They must have felt they were playing a game of Whack-A-Mole. They could never get in front of the disease. Christina was a reminder to them of their limitations. I won't even get into the doctors in the other lesser categories. Nothing is to be gained.

Eventually the attacks continued to progress down her body. Her bladder shut down and she had to catheterize herself twice a day to urinate. She developed pancreatitis which caused excruciating pain. Then the infections started. These were very serious. It was not until a brand new antibiotic was used that they were finally slowed down. Finally the disease went after her intestines and colon. By this time she had to be under 80 pounds, but she refused to tell anyone what she weighed.

Christmas of 2016 was to be her final Christmas, and I think she knew it. She had it all planned out. She got dressed up and put on makeup. She looked the very best she could, but at 80 pounds, she was a shadow of her former self. We went to Mass on Christmas Day at Holy Cross. She was too weak to walk all the way out of church after Mass. She sat in the last pew while I got the car. Aaron and I helped her walk to it and get inside. Christmas dinner was to be a family tradition, prime rib with Yorkshire pudding. Jen prepared the beef and side dishes. My specialty was the Yorkshire pudding. I developed a way to make them gluten free for her, and she thoroughly enjoyed them. So much so, that I made them again the following day. Several times in the weeks before Christmas she remarked to Aaron and me that she wanted to have a last family picture taken on Christmas day. After dinner, Christina, Aaron, Jen and I posed for the picture. She passed away 20 days later on January 14, 2017.

The Final Picture

THE COFFEE SHOP

I MUST HAVE ZONED OUT FOR some period of time thinking about Christina. When I mentally returned to the coffee shop, I remember the jerk across from me going on about how if Christina never existed how much more money I would have today. The cost of caring for her, her education, her wedding and all of the little things would suddenly show up in my bank account. The pain and suffering that Jennifer, Aaron, and I were going through, as well as that of all the others who'd known her, would be gone. Opportunities like this don't come by often, if at all. I would be the ultimate sucker if I didn't jump at the opportunity he was presenting.

I did my best to ignore him, but he persisted. I found myself wondering if his boss could make someone go away, disappear, never exist, why didn't he do it with people like Hitler, Stalin or that sadistic savage in North Korea. These folks and people like them truly put evil, misery and suffering in the world. They have no socially redeeming value. The world would be much better if they had never existed. Then it hit me. I knew who his boss was. He did not want to erase people like them. They served his purpose. He couldn't go after people like Mother Theresa because she was too big and too popular. I am sure he tried to derail her along her path to sainthood, but he couldn't erase her after she

51

Printed in the United States
By Bookmasters